The universe, a vast expanse,
A cosmic dance of time and chance,
A canvas painted with cosmic light,
A wonderland beyond our sight.

From the tiniest particle to the largest star,
The universe stretches near and far,
A tapestry woven with cosmic threads,
A cosmic mystery that lies ahead.

The galaxies spin in endless dance,
A cosmic waltz with elegance,
Each star a spark of cosmic fire,
A beacon in the cosmic choir.

And in this cosmic symphony,
We find ourselves a part of the harmony,
A small speck in a vast expanse,
A cosmic miracle of chance.

For in the universe we find,
A beauty that astounds the mind,
A universe of endless grace,
A cosmic wonderland to embrace.

Our galaxy, a spiral of light,
A cosmic beacon in the night,
A swirling mass of stars and dust,
A cosmic wonder that we trust.

From the center, a bright light shines,
A supermassive black hole that confines,
The mysteries of our galactic core,
A cosmic riddle to explore.

The arms of our galaxy stretch wide,
A cosmic dance with grace and pride,
Each star a spark of cosmic fire,
A beacon in the galactic choir.

And in this cosmic symphony,
We find ourselves a part of the harmony,
A small speck in a vast expanse,
A cosmic miracle of chance.

For in our galaxy we find,
A beauty that astounds the mind,
A universe of endless grace,
A cosmic wonderland to embrace.

So let us marvel at the stars,
And ponder what lies beyond afar,
For in our galaxy we see,
A glimpse of the divine mystery.

Depression, a weight so heavy to bear,
A darkness that looms, a constant despair,
A battle within, a relentless snare,
A life in turmoil, a never-ending scare.

Days without end, a numbness so deep,
A void inside, a heart that won't keep,
A shattered soul, a mind that won't sleep,
A constant ache, that makes one weep.

The world so bleak, no light to see,
A constant struggle, to simply be,
A life in ruins, a desperate plea,
To break free from this agony.

But hope remains, though faint at first,
A glimmer of light, a sense of thirst,
For something more, something to burst,
The bubble of darkness, to quench the worst.

With time and care, and help from friends,
A path to healing, a new life begins,
Slowly at first, but then it mends,
The broken pieces, that depression rends.

So hold on, dear one, don't give up the fight,
You're not alone, in this endless night,
There's always hope, there's always light,
To break free from depression's might.

Winter's beauty, a wonder to behold,
A snowy landscape, a story untold,
The warmth of love, a treasure to hold,
Winter's beauty, a season of gold.

The crisp, cold air, a refreshing breeze,
A world transformed, a canvas to please,
The cozy hearth, a place of ease,
Winter's beauty, a moment of peace.

The glittering snow, a shimmering veil,
A world of white, a fairy tale,
The loving embrace, a warm detail,
Winter's beauty, a season to prevail.

The sun sets, a glorious sight,
A stunning display, a canvas so bright,
The sky ablaze, with hues so right,
A breathtaking moment, before the night.

The clouds aglow, with golden rays,
A fiery ball, a farewell blaze,
The beauty it brings, a soulful craze,
A mesmerizing view, that forever stays.

The moon, a silver orb in the sky,
A beacon for the lost and shy,
It casts a gentle, glowing light,
And fills our hearts with wonder bright.

It waxes and it wanes each night,
A constant source of changing sight,
A symbol of the passing days,
A reminder of life's fleeting ways.

Oh moon, how lovely you appear,
So close and yet so far, so near,
You shine upon us from above,
And fill our souls with peace and love.

Kolibris, oh Kolibris,
Fluttering wings with such ease,
A flash of color, a blur of motion,
A sight to behold, a wondrous notion.

Tiny creatures of nature's design,
Drinking nectar, so sweet and fine,
Dancing in the air, with grace and skill,
A marvel of flight, a joyful thrill.

Their beaks like needles, so precise,
Piercing flowers, like a lover's kiss,
Extracting the nectar, so pure and sweet,
A feast for their bodies, a wondrous treat.

Kolibris, oh Kolibris,
A symbol of beauty, a symbol of bliss,
A reminder of nature's boundless grace,
A treasure of life, in this wondrous place.

A butterfly flaps its wings,
And sets off a chain of things,
A tiny movement, so small and light,
Yet it can change the world with its flight.

Friendship is a bond that's hard to break,
A connection that's strong and hard to fake.
It's a relationship based on trust and care,
A bond that's built to last and always be there.

Friends are there to share in the joys of life,
To celebrate and laugh through every strife.
They offer comfort and a listening ear,
And wipe away every single tear.

Friends are there to offer a helping hand,
To stand by your side and always understand.
They lift us up when we're feeling down,
And bring us back to solid ground.

True friendship is a treasure that's rare,
A bond that's built on love and care.
It's a connection that's meant to last,
A bond that's stronger than any cast.

So cherish your friends and hold them tight,
For they bring warmth and light to life.
And always remember, through thick and thin,
True friendship will always win.

In the dark abyss where shadows lie,

A weary soul prepares to die,

A tender heart, a shattered dream,

Lost in the void, a silent scream.

Whispers of hope, a fleeting glance,

A moment's pause, a serenade dance,

But shadows grow and consume the light,

Engulfing all in the blackest night.

Shackled by chains of despair and pain,

A soul cries out, longing to break the chain,

For where once love and laughter thrived,

Now only anguish and torment reside.

The crimson river, it gently flows,

A final release, a graceful bow,

As fragile petals fall from the sky,

The sun dips low, a last goodbye.

In the hearts of those who've been left behind,

A haunting memory, a tearful sigh,

A plea for forgiveness, a search for the truth,

A shattered world in the wake of youth.

Oh, weary soul, if only you knew,

The love and warmth that surrounded you,

In this life, a fleeting breath,

A moment's pause before eternal rest.

But let the skies weep and the winds wail,

For the story's end, a tragic tale,

And as the stars weep and the moon weeps,

In the arms of the night, a soul finds peace.

In the heart of a world enshrouded,

Where shadows drape the weary land,

A glint of hope, resilient and undoubted,

Sows seeds of love with a gentle hand.

The stars above, they whisper and wink,

Their secrets told to the dark expanse,

A symphony of hope, an eternal link,

Guiding the lost in an endless dance.

Through the veil of obsidian skies,

A ray of light pierces the shroud,

A beacon of hope, a phoenix rise,

In the silent night, it sings aloud.

In the depths of despair, we stumble and fall,

Yet a whisper of hope, its voice so clear,

Urges us forward, to rise and crawl,

To face our fears, our path to steer.

With each step, the darkness wanes,

The glow of hope illuminates our way,

An ember of love, it breaks the chains,

That bind us to the night, leading us astray.

In the arms of hope, we find our solace,

A sanctuary where weary hearts beat,

Together we rise, hand in hand, embrace,

The power of love, a force complete.

In a world of shadows, of blackened night,

Hope's guiding light prevails and shines,

A beacon that leads us through the fight,

To a realm of love, where darkness resigns.

In the vast expanse of time and space,

Where stars align and fates entwine,

A fragile miracle takes its place,

The precious gift of life, divine.

Upon this sphere of azure hues,

Amidst the chaos, life unveils,

The heartbeat's song, the morning's dews,

A symphony of love prevails.

The fabric of existence, spun,

Intricate patterns, interlaced,

Each thread of life, a setting sun,

A fleeting glimpse of beauty, graced.

In every breath, a moment's chance,

To taste the wonders life bestows,

To feel the rhythm of life's dance,

In every sigh and tear that flows.

The heart, a vessel for love's embrace,

Boundless and pure, a beacon bright,

A refuge in the tempest's gale,

A solace in the darkest night.

For life is but a fleeting breath,

A fragile thread, a transient spark,

A brief encounter with love and death,

A journey through the light and dark.

In the end, when shadows fall,

And time begins to fade away,

The echoes of our lives enthrall,

The memories that forever stay.

Embrace the gift, this fleeting dream,

Hold tight to love, and dare to soar,

For life's but a whisper on the wind,

A sacred dance on fate's vast floor.

In the tapestry of life, we weave,

A story of love, of joy and pain,

The essence of our lives, believe,

In every heartbeat, life's refrain.

In a realm where hearts entwine,

A tale of love, pure and divine,

Two souls embarked on a sacred quest,

To find a haven, where love finds rest.

With tender touch and gentle gaze,

They danced through life's bewildering maze,

Love's tapestry they began to weave,

With threads of trust and bonds that won't leave.

They nurtured a garden of dreams and desires,

Watered with affection that never tires,

Each word spoken, a soothing balm,

In their embrace, they found eternal calm.

Through stormy seas and darkened skies,

They stood together, side by side,

Their love a lighthouse, shining bright,

Guiding them through the darkest night.

In laughter shared and tears embraced,

They discovered love's unending grace,

For love, you see, is not a mere act,

But a symphony played by hearts, intact.

They listened, understood, and cared,

In every triumph, every tear they shared,

Their love a shelter from the world's disdain,

A refuge where vulnerability found no pain.

They cherished moments, both big and small,

Building a fortress where love stood tall,

And within this fortress, they found solace,

A sanctuary where love was boundless.

For love, my friend, is not mere chance,

But a choice to embark on life's dance,

To hold another's heart with utmost care,

And in that embrace, find joy so rare.

In the cool, clear waters of the stream,

The salmon swim, their scales agleam,

Their journey long, their mission clear,

To return home, to spawn each year.

Against the current they push and fight,

Their bodies strong, their wills so bright,

Upstream they go, against the flow,

To reach their goal, where they must go.

Their journey's end, within their sight,

They leap up high, with all their might,

To clear the falls, and reach the pool,

Where they will spawn, and life renew.

Their work complete, they fade away,

Their offspring now, will have their day,

To swim and grow, in the cool, clear stream,

And continue the cycle, like a dream.

In fields of green and sun-kissed earth,

Amidst the trees and gentle breeze,

A wondrous sight of vibrant mirth,

As flowers bloom with effortless ease.

Their petals soft and delicate,

Unfurling in the morning sun,

Their colors bold and passionate,

A symphony of beauty begun.

From daisies white to roses red,

And everything in between,

Each one a gift to heart and head,

A sight to make the soul serene.

With every petal, every hue,

They speak of life and hope and joy,

And as they bloom, so do we too,

With peace and love that knows no coy.

In the golden dawn of a summer's embrace,

The world awakens with a radiant grace.

The sun, a fiery ball, ascends the sky,

Painting the horizon in hues that fly.

The air, so crisp, now carries a sweet song,

As birds harmonize, melodious and strong.

Leaves dance with joy upon each gentle breeze,

Whispering secrets among the swaying trees.

The meadows bloom in a vibrant array,

Where wildflowers dance, a colorful ballet.

Their petals reach out, as if to embrace,

The warm caress of sunlight's tender

Behold the vast expanse of the seas,

A realm of wonder, a world of mysteries.

Where azure waves dance with the sun's caress,

And whispers of the tides bring gentle finesse.

Beneath the surface, a realm unseen,

A kaleidoscope of life, vibrant and serene.

Coral reefs adorned with colors so bright,

Where creatures of the deep take their graceful flight.

The oceans, they hold ancient tales,

Of legends untold, of forgotten trails.

They carry the whispers of seafarers' dreams,

And the secrets of sunken ships, lost it seems.

From the playful dance of dolphins' delight,

To the majestic might of the whale's grand height,

The oceans teem with creatures wild and free,

A symphony of life, an ode to the sea.

They cradle the moon's silver reflection,

A liquid mirror of celestial connection.

With every crashing wave and foaming crest,

They sing a timeless hymn, a song of unrest.

Yet the oceans, they yearn for our care,

Their beauty endangered, a plea in the air.

Let's be guardians of this watery domain,

Preserving its splendor, erasing the stain.

For in the oceans, a tapestry unfolds,

A sanctuary for creatures, young and old.

Let us protect this fragile, wondrous place,

Embrace its grace with love and embrace.

In twilight's embrace, fireflies ignite,
A dazzling dance, a magical sight.
Their flickering glow, a gentle embrace,
Enchanting the night, leaving no trace.

In the grandeur of towering heights,
Mountains rise, majestic sights.
Their peaks touch the sky, proud and bold,
A testament to nature's power untold.

Under the silver glow of the moon,

A serenade unfolds, a melodic boon.

Whispers of love carried on moonbeams,

A nocturnal symphony, woven in dreams.

From slumber's grip, the earth awakes,

Spring's gentle touch, new life it makes.

Blossoms bloom in vibrant array,

A celebration of rebirth, a joyous display.

In winter's hush, the world stands still,

A blanket of snow, serene and chill.

The air is crisp, the silence profound,

A moment of peace, where tranquility is found.

The waves crash upon the shore,

Whispers of the sea forevermore.

Their rhythm soothes the weary soul,

A timeless melody, making us whole.

Leaves of crimson and gold adorn the trees,

A tapestry of beauty, autumn's masterpiece.

They dance and twirl in the crisp, cool air,

A fiery embrace before winter's affair.

From cloudy skies, a teardrop falls,

A raindrop's journey, as it softly calls.

It kisses the earth, quenching its thirst,

A gift from above, a nature's verse.

In the velvet canvas of the night,

Stars ignite, a celestial sight.

They twinkle and shimmer, oh so bright,

Guiding dreamers through the darkest plight.

© 2023 Joakim Nurminen
Kustantaja: BoD – Books on Demand, Helsinki, Suomi
Valmistaja: BoD – Books on Demand, Norderstedt, Saksa
ISBN: 978-952-33-0163-4